WONDERFUL
WORLD OF
ANIMALS

For a free color catalog describing Gareth Stevens' list of high-quality books and multimedia programs, call 1-800-542-2595 (USA) or 1-800-461-9120 (Canada). Gareth Stevens Publishing's Fax: (414) 225-0377.
See our catalog, too, on the World Wide Web: http://gsinc.com

Library of Congress Cataloging-in-Publication Data

MacLeod, Beatrice.
    Fish / text by Beatrice MacLeod ; illustrated by Matteo Chesi.
      p. cm. -- (Wonderful world of animals)
    Includes bibliographical references (p. 31) and index.
    Summary: Introduces the physical characteristics, behavior, and habitat
of various fish.
    ISBN 0-8368-1955-1 (lib. bdg.)
    1. Fishes--Juvenile literature. [1. Fishes.] I. Chesi, Matteo, ill.
II. Title. III. Series: MacLeod, Beatrice. Wonderful world of animals.
QL617.2.M335 1997
597--dc21   97-19504

This North American edition first published in 1997 by
Gareth Stevens Publishing
1555 North RiverCenter Drive, Suite 201
Milwaukee, Wisconsin 53212 USA

This U.S. edition © 1997 by Gareth Stevens, Inc. Created and produced with original © 1996 by McRae Books Srl, Via dei Rustici, 5 - Florence, Italy. Additional end matter © 1997 by Gareth Stevens, Inc.

Text: Beatrice MacLeod
Design: Marco Nardi
Illustrations: Matteo Chesi
U.S. Editor: Patricia Lantier-Sampon
Editorial assistants: Diane Laska, Rita Reitci

Note: Beatrice MacLeod has a Bachelor of Science degree in Biology. She works as a freelance journalist for Italian nature magazines and also writes children's nonfiction books on nature.

Printed in the United States of America

1 2 3 4 5 6 7 8 9 01 00 99 98 97

WONDERFUL WORLD OF ANIMALS

FISH

Text by Beatrice MacLeod
Illustrated by Matteo Chesi

Gareth Stevens Publishing
MILWAUKEE

WHAT IS A FISH?

All fish live in water. They nearly all breathe through gills and have scales and fins. Scientists divide fish into three groups: jawless fish, cartilaginous fish, and bony fish.

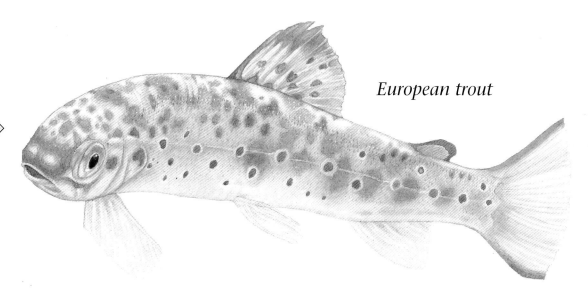

European trout

Trout are part of the class of bony fish. This is by far the largest group. Bony fish have skeletons of bone and a bony cover over their gills. Their scales are also made of thin, overlapping plates of bone.

Blue shark

Sharks
are part of the
cartilaginous class.
Their bones are made of
cartilage, which is a firm
elastic material. Skates and
rays are also members of
this group.

Lampreys are jawless
fish. They have
smooth, eel-like
bodies and
jawless sucking
Lamprey   mouths with horny teeth. Jawless fish,
which also include hagfish, are the
most primitive types of fish alive today.

FISH HOMES

The first fish lived over 450 million years ago. Since then, they have evolved in many different ways and have colonized every aquatic habitat in the world.

Pike live in lakes and rivers. They sometimes grow to over 3 feet (1 meter) in length. They are common game fish and fierce hunters.

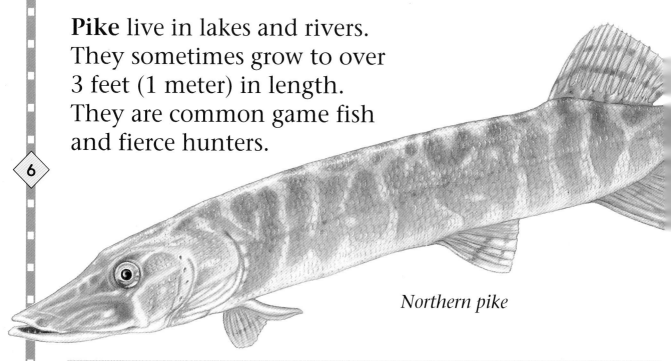

Northern pike

Studying fish
The science of studying fish is called **ichthyology**, from the Greek word *ichthys*, which means "fish." The Ancient Greeks, especially the famous philosopher Aristotle, knew a lot about fish.

Swordfish

Swordfish live in tropical oceans. They are unusual because of the long, pointed sword on the end of their snout. They use this sword as a weapon when hunting. Swordfish can weigh as much as 1,500 pounds (680 kilograms).

7

SPECIAL HOMES

Some fish live in special habitats and have evolved physical features that help them survive there. These can include being bright or dull in color to blend in with the background. Some deep-water fish produce light to attract prey or mates. The salmon spends one part of its life in fresh water and another part in salt water at sea.

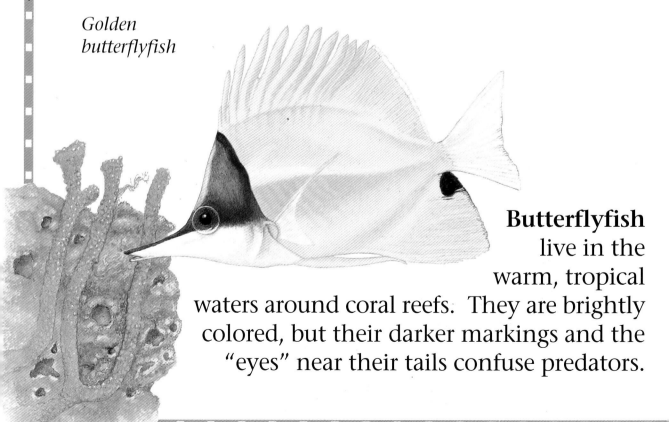

Golden butterflyfish

Butterflyfish live in the warm, tropical waters around coral reefs. They are brightly colored, but their darker markings and the "eyes" near their tails confuse predators.

Salmon begin their lives in freshwater streams. They spend several years in these waters before migrating to the sea. After four or five years at sea, they journey back upriver to spawn their own young and begin the cycle over again.

Atlantic salmon

9

Angler fish live in the ocean depths. They have huge heads and mouths. Many have a luminous organ, called an esca, on their heads. The esca acts as bait to attract the fish they like to eat.

Angler fish

FISH OUT OF WATER

Some fish can survive out of the water. Flying fish skim above the water for short distances. Other fish use their fins to walk or slither along on land. Breathing is the biggest problem for a fish out of water. Some, like the mudskipper, store water in their gills and breathe from this. Only a few species can breathe directly from the air.

Mudskippers live in swamps, estuaries, and mud flats in tropical regions. They walk on land using their pectoral fins.

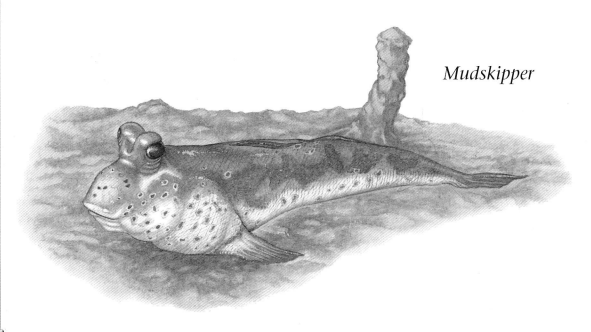

Mudskipper

Flying gunard

Flying gunards leap out of the water and "fly" along above the surface for a few yards. They usually do this to escape a predator.

Tiny **hatchet fish** beat their fins quickly and propel themselves along. They skim across the surface of the water with their deep chests for about 40 feet (12 m).

Hatchet fish

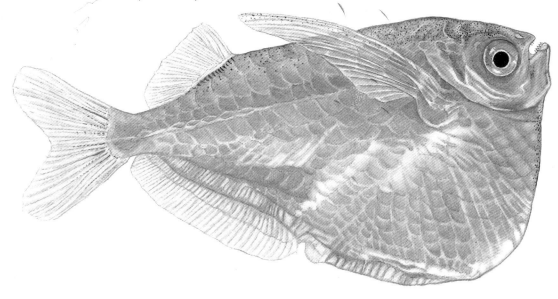

FIERCE FISH

Most fish feed on invertebrates and other fish smaller than themselves. Although most carnivorous fish (meat-eaters) have teeth, they use them only for holding prey, which they swallow whole. Some fish, such as sharks and piranhas, have cutting teeth for biting chunks out of their victims. A smaller number of fish are herbivores (plant-eaters).

Piranha

Piranhas live together in shoals. They have short, powerful jaws with razor-sharp teeth. They feed as a group. A feeding frenzy may be set off by blood in the water. A victim can be eaten up in just a few minutes.

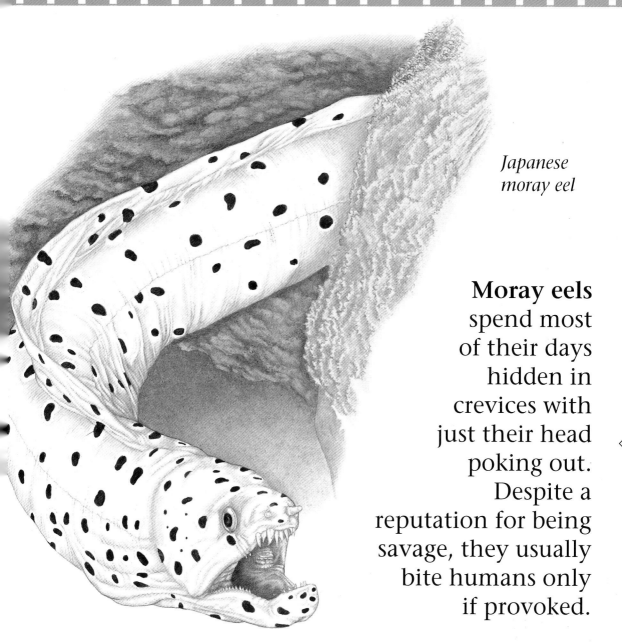

Japanese moray eel

Moray eels spend most of their days hidden in crevices with just their head poking out. Despite a reputation for being savage, they usually bite humans only if provoked.

The piranha – a fish with a bad reputation
A famous story tells about a man and a horse who fell into a river where piranhas lived. Their bones were found just a few hours later picked entirely clean of flesh. The man's clothes were undamaged.

SEA GIANTS

Fish come in all shapes and sizes. Dwarf goby are the smallest marine fish. They grow to only about 0.4 inch (1 centimeter) long. But some fish in Earth's oceans are huge!

Mantas and **stingrays** can grow to enormous sizes. The Atlantic devil ray is the largest of all the living species. It can weigh up to 2 tons.

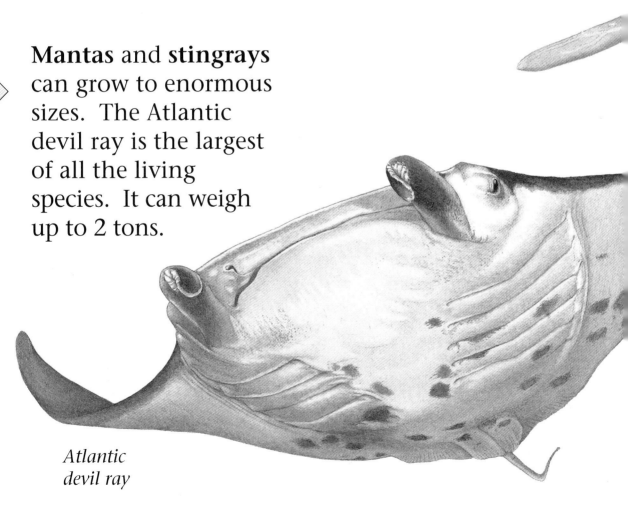

Atlantic devil ray

*Whale shark
and plankton*

The **whale shark** is the largest fish of all.
It can grow as long as 40 feet (12 m).
Despite its huge size, it is quite harmless
and eats plankton. It lives in warm parts
of the Atlantic, Pacific, and Indian oceans.

What is plankton?

Plankton is a collective name for tiny organisms
that drift in the water. They are very important
because many fish, birds, and mammals feed on
them. They are the basis of the aquatic food chain.

SKILLFUL HUNTERS

Catching the next meal sometimes calls for some skillful moves. Many fish have highly specialized hunting techniques. These can include leaping out of the water to grab an insect, or even shooting it off a branch.

Electric rays spend most of their time drowsing peacefully on the seafloor. But when they are hungry, they wake up and blast the fish around them with a strong electric shock. The fish are stunned and easy to catch.

Electric ray

Teeth and diet

A fish's mouth gives important clues about what it eats. For example, predators have pointed, cutting teeth, and coral-eaters have stubby, strong teeth. Some fish have teeth in their throat and none in their mouth.

Archer fish are skilled marksmen. They lie in wait under plants hanging over the water. When an insect lands on a plant, the fish knocks it off its perch by shooting a series of water droplets at it. Archer fish can hit their target from 2-3 feet (60-90 cm) away. Once they hit the insect, they don't wait for it to drop off into the water where other fish might eat it. Instead, they leap up and grab the insect before it hits the surface.

Archer fish

REPRODUCTION

The majority of fish lay hundreds or even thousands of eggs in the water, which hatch after a few days or weeks. Many of these eggs are eaten by other fish before they hatch. Only a few fish give birth to live young.

Most species of **sharks** give birth to live young. The eggs are fertilized and develop inside the female, in much the same way as mammals.

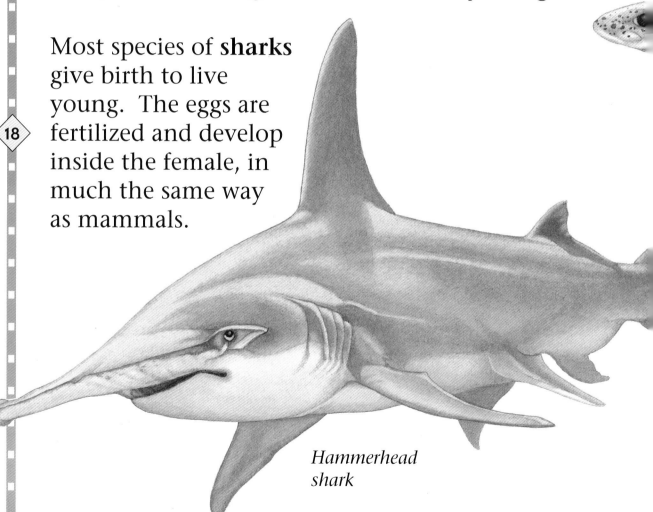

*Hammerhead
shark*

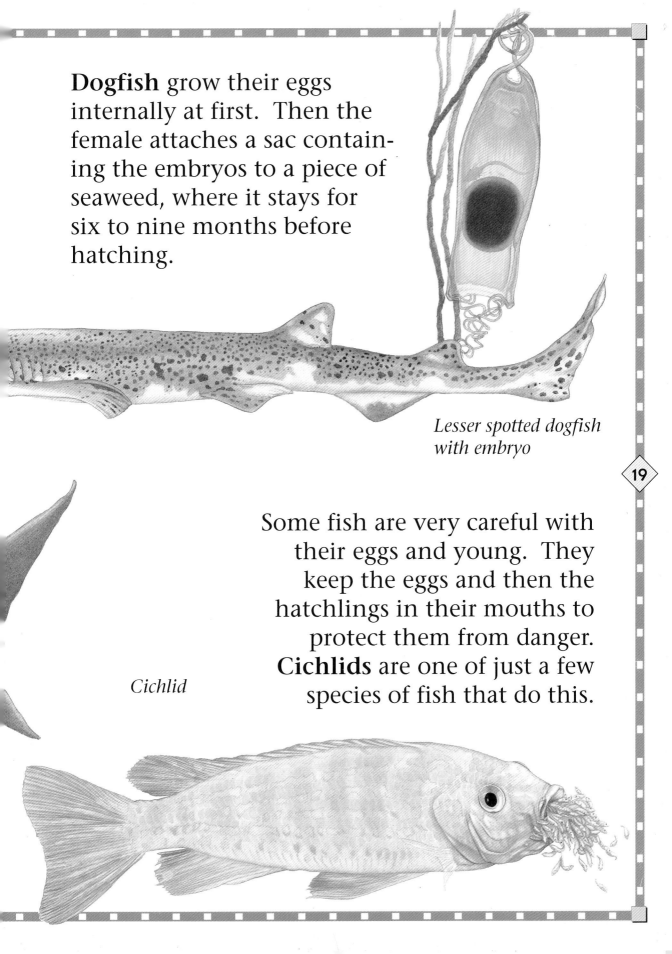

Dogfish grow their eggs internally at first. Then the female attaches a sac containing the embryos to a piece of seaweed, where it stays for six to nine months before hatching.

Lesser spotted dogfish with embryo

Some fish are very careful with their eggs and young. They keep the eggs and then the hatchlings in their mouths to protect them from danger. **Cichlids** are one of just a few species of fish that do this.

Cichlid

WORKING TOGETHER

Fish that share a habitat sometimes have a special relationship that benefits one or both of them. They may protect one another from predators, help keep one or the other clean, or provide each other with food.

Anemone clownfish

Anemone clownfish live safely among the poisonous tentacles of the sea anemone. They are immune to the anemone's poison and are safe from predators.

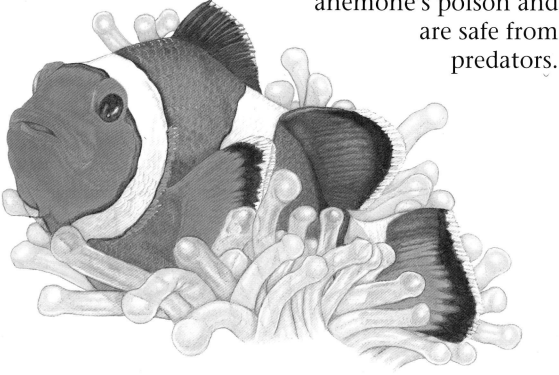

Grouper with blue-and-white goby cleaner fish at work in its mouth

Tiny **cleaner fish** apparently risk their lives inside the mouths of bigger fish. But it is not as dangerous as it looks. The cleaner fish eat parasites and damaged tissue inside. Both fish benefit since one gets a meal and the other gets a clean-up job.

Getting along

When two animals live together in harmony and both species receive benefits, the relationship is called *symbiotic*. If only one animal benefits and the other is harmed, the relationship is called *parasitic*.

ARE THESE ALL FISH?

The word *fish* is a very general term. It groups animals together that are less closely related than, for example, a sparrow and an elephant. The animals on these two pages are all unusual fish.

Porcupine fish

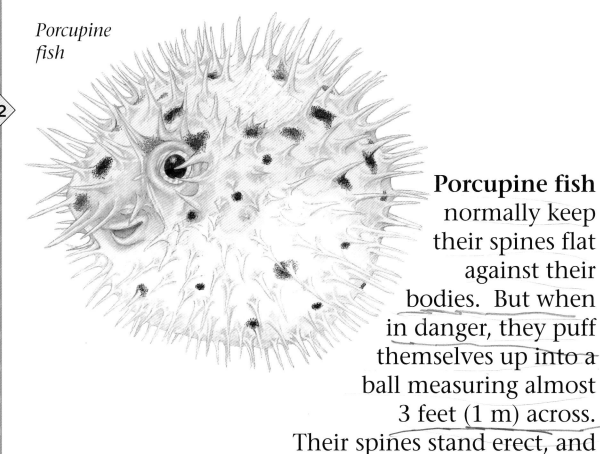

Porcupine fish normally keep their spines flat against their bodies. But when in danger, they puff themselves up into a ball measuring almost 3 feet (1 m) across. Their spines stand erect, and predators are afraid to come near.

Sea horses swim in an upright position. They use their dorsal fin to propel themselves through the water. At breeding time, the female lays her eggs (about 200) in a pouch near the male's tail. After about two months, the male expels a large brood of tiny, transparent sea horses.

Sea horse

Although it looks very different, the **pipe-fish** is a close relative of the sea horse. It has the same tubelike snout, its body is covered in armor, and the male also has a pouch near the tail in which the female lays her eggs. Color and pattern vary according to species to help the fish blend into their environment.

Pipe-fish

FISH ON THE MOVE

Most fish stay in groups called schools, or shoals. This tricks predators into thinking they are a huge, single individual and discourages these predators from attacking. Only a few of the larger fish species travel great distances to hunt prey. Some species migrate many thousands of miles to find the right conditions for breeding.

Sardines are part of the herring family. They live in dense schools and feed along the coasts in seas and oceans around the world. While their shoaling habits are a defense against predators, it makes them easy prey for fishermen's nets.

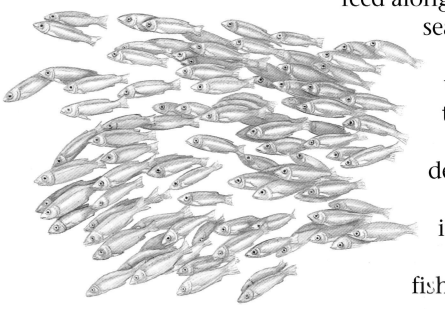

A built-in compass?

Salmon migrate long distances to breed. Scientists aren't certain how these fish find their way back to the waters of their birth. It may be instinct, sensitivity to ocean currents, or to Earth's magnetic field. They may follow the Sun, or a special odor, or have a sort of internal compass.

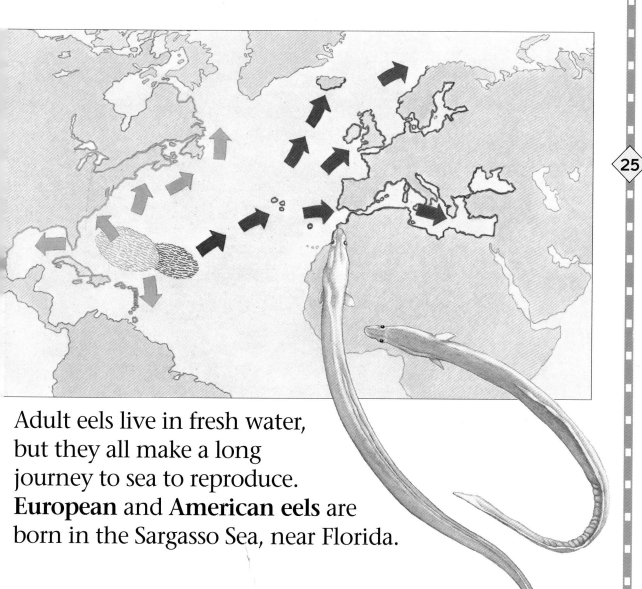

Adult eels live in fresh water, but they all make a long journey to sea to reproduce. **European** and **American eels** are born in the Sargasso Sea, near Florida.

THE STRANGEST FISH!

Many animals develop extraordinary adaptations to help them survive. Some fish look like plants or rocks, others have long whiskers, and still others rest on leg-like fins. Anything goes when life itself is at stake!

Many **scorpion fish** have flaps, projections, spines, and folds on their bodies that make them look like the rocks on the sea bottom where they live. Many species are highly poisonous.

Scorpion fish

Many species of **catfish** have long whiskers, called barbels. The barbels are very sensitive and help the fish locate food on the seafloor.

Catfish

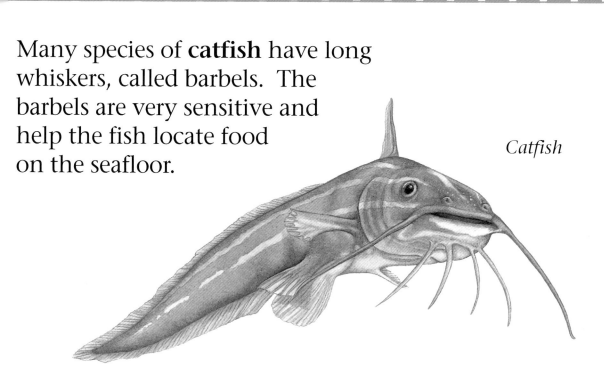

Some fish live in the oceans' depths, where the water is dark and cold. **Tripod fish** live on the ocean floor as deep as 19,000 feet (5,800 m). They rest on their stiffened pelvic fins with their pectoral fins raised over their head, pointing into the current.

Tripod fish

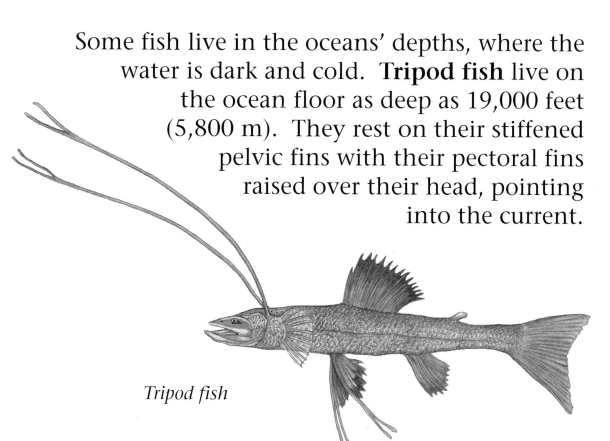

Glossary

adaptations: changes or adjustments made in order to survive in a changing environment.

anemones: animals without skeletons that live in the ocean, usually attached to rocks and shells and feeding on plankton they catch with their tentacles.

aquatic: of or relating to water; living or growing in water.

breed *(v)*: When male and female animals join together, or mate, to produce young.

colonize: to set up a group or community where all members live or work together.

crevices: narrow openings or cracks in rock.

dorsal fin: the fin on the center back of a fish.

environment: the surroundings in which plants, animals, and other organisms live.

estuary: where the sea meets the mouth of a river.

evolve: to change shape or develop gradually from one form to another. Over time, all living things must evolve to survive in their changing environments, or they may become extinct.

fertilize: adding male sex cells to the female egg to start the growth and development of a new individual.

gills: the breathing organs in all fish; also called branchiae.

habitat: the natural home of a plant or animal.

28

hatchlings: newly hatched fish.

immune: having a resistance to or not affected by something.

invertebrates: animals without a backbone.

luminous: having light; giving out a steady glow.

marine: relating to the sea.

migrate: to move from one place or climate to another, usually on a seasonal basis.

pectoral fins: fins located on the sides of a fish behind the gills.

pelvic fins: a pair of fins on a fish's belly located between the head and the tail.

philosopher: a scholar; a thinker; one who searches for wisdom.

predators: animals that kill and eat other animals.

prey: animals that are hunted and killed for food by other animals.

primitive: of or relating to an early and usually simple stage of development.

spawn *(v)*: to release eggs in water.

tentacles: narrow, flexible parts or limbs that certain animals use for moving around or catching prey.

transparent: letting light pass through so that objects can be seen on the other side.

tropical: belonging to the tropics, or the region centered on the equator and lying between the Tropic of Cancer (23.5 degrees north of the equator) and the Tropic of Capricorn (23.5 degrees south of the equator). This region is typically very hot and humid.

ACTIVITIES

1. A good way to find out about fish is to keep one as a pet. One or more goldfish would be a good start. Someone at the store in which you buy your goldfish and its supplies can tell you how to care for your new pet. He or she should also be able to explain how to keep tropical fish. How do people care for fish that need to stay in saltwater? What is a balanced aquarium, and what do you need in order to have one?

2. Make a scrapbook of different kinds of fish by cutting out and pasting in pictures of fish from old magazines. You might want to put the fish pictures in groups, such as all the tropical fish together, or all the cold climate fish on the same pages. If you know the name of the fish, print it neatly next to its picture. Another way to get pictures is to ask a grownup to help you photocopy them from a library book. You can color your photocopies with crayons, color pencils, or watercolor paints. Paint wavy blue and green lines between the pictures to make waves.

3. Ask your parents to take you for a visit to a public aquarium and study the various kinds of fish on display. What other kinds of animals does the aquarium keep? Must some kinds of fish be kept separate from other kinds? Why do you think this is necessary? Look for the kinds of fish that thrive in the wild in your geographical region or area. Learn their names and remember what they look like. The next time you see fish in the wild in a lake or a river, try to identify them.

BOOKS AND VIDEOS

Amazing Fish. Mary Ling (Knopf Books)

The Aquarium Take-along Book. Sheldon L. Gerstenfeld (Puffin Books)

Colors of the Sea series. Eric Ethan (Gareth Stevens)

Crinkleroot's 25 Fish Every Child Should Know. Jim Arnoski (Simon and Schuster)

Dragons and Rainbow Runners: Exploring Fish with Children. Suzanne Samson (Rinehart, Roberts)

Extremely Weird Fishes. Sarah Lovett (John Muir)

Fearsome Fish. Steve Parker (Raintree/Steck-Vaughn)

Fish. (AIMS Media video)

Fish Are Interesting. (Phoenix/BFA Films and Video)

Fish: Swimming and Floating. Isidro Sánchez (Gareth Stevens)

Sea Fish, Shellfish and Other Underwater Life. (TMW Media Group video)

Secrets of the Animal World series. (Gareth Stevens)

Surprising Swimmers. Anthony D. Fredericks (NorthWord)

The World of Fish. (Kimbo Educational video)

WEB SITES

www.wh.whoi.edu/homepage/faq.html

http://pathfinder.com/@@ZMM3AQA8ryUWn@b/_
  pathfinder/kidstuff/underwater/album/album.html

INDEX